Maria McManus is a poet and playwright. She was born in 1964 in Enniskillen, Co. Fermanagh, and she was educated at the University of Ulster and Queens University, Belfast, where she completed a MA in creative writing.

She has been published in various anthologies including *Introductions 1* (Lagan, 2004), and *The Lonely Poets' Guide to Belfast* (New Belfast Community Arts Initiative, 2002).

She is the inaugural winner of the Bedell Scholarship for Literature and World Citizenship 2005 awarded by the Aspen Writers' Foundation, Colorado.

Her theatre credits include *His 'n' Hers*, co-written with Ray Scannell and produced in 2005 by Replay Theatre Company and *The Black-Out Show* for Red Lead Arts. *Nowhere Harder* was developed and performed as part of Replay Theatre Company's Script Lab in the Belfast Festival at Queen's in 2003.

Maria lives in Strangford Co. Down with her husband and daughters.

READING THE DOG

April 2007.

for Mary

Enjoy **READING THE DOG**

MARIA McMANUS

LAGAN PRESS
BELFAST
2006

Acknowledgements
Some of these poems, or versions of them, first appeared in
Introductions 1 (Lagan 2004), *Black Mountain Review, Fortnight* and
*The Lonely Poets' Guide to Belfast (New Belfast Community Arts
Initiative).*

In 'On Hatfield Street', *'one stone more, a pure stone, that the river
bears away' (page 47) is quoted from* 'Oh Earth, Wait for Me' *as
translated from Pablo Neruda's* 'Oh Thierra Esperamé' *by Anthony
Kerrigan. On page 49, lines reference Paul Muldoon's* 'Party Piece' *and*
'Postscript' *by Seamus Heaney.* 'Whatever you say say nothing', *is from
the poem of the same name by Seamus Heaney.*

'Alternative Ulster' (page 33) *and* 'Suspect Device' (page 36) *and the
title of the poem* 'Inflammable Material' *are all references to songs by
Stiff Little Fingers.* 'Blockbuster', *by The Sweet is quoted on page 33.*

Published by
Lagan Press
1A Bryson Street
Belfast BT5 4ES
e-mail: lagan-press@e-books.org.uk
web: lagan-press.org.uk

ARTS
COUNCIL
of Northern Ireland

ISBN: 1 904652 35 2
Author: McManus, Maria
Title: Reading the Dog
2006

Design: December
Printed by J.H. Haynes, Sparkford

'He was born invisible. His mother was invisible too, and that was why she could see him. His people lived contented lives, working on farms, under the familiar sunlight. Their lives stretched back into the invisible centuries and all that had come down from those differently coloured ages were legends and rich traditions, unwritten and therefore remembered. They were remembered because they were lived.'

—Ben Okri, *Astonishing the Gods*

for Kevin, Aislín and Orla

Contents

The Nature of Forgiveness

I

Talk to me
about the nature of forgiveness.
The letting go of wrongs done
would startle
the face of God
in the open-mouthed petals
of a late iris
in voiceless song;

this terrible fear
of fractured friendships
and all the risk of loving people anyway.

A shock of Honesty,
empty of seeds,
its pearly membranes give colour
to the dull dun thorn hedge,
contrast over the verdant grass, even when
long past its own purple blossom.

There is something of the conflict of a sex blown open—
alive, wild like a heart, and everything
it takes to shut that down.

And this obsession with death—
a mesmerising dislocation
about what will happen next.

Speak to me. We are celebrating
passion. I am uninjured.

II
Feast Days

The parish bulletin
marked out feast days for fasting.

There was nothing else to read
in my Nanny Hegarty's house
except the Bible,
the *Sacred Heart Messenger*
& the *St. Martin de Porres Magazine*—

Nothing to play with, but a mangle.

I learned about
the patron saint of debts

and terminal illness.

III
Displacement

I robbed the spring banks
of primroses and bluebells for a May Altar.
There were only daisies otherwise.

There was nothing in the gardens of my childhood
that was not wild,
that was not laden with the Cuckoo Flower,
Herb Robert,
feathered grasses, seeds, and the sudden dun-white flash

of sparring hares
in fields fringed with bulrushes,
reeds, cygnets, and later,
all summer,
dragonflies.

I lived in a world up close:
the peat-rich water,
the riverbanks,
poppies, crab apple,
blackthorn,

foxgloves, heart-stopping foxgloves,
pale wild roses, harebells—

everything that wilted quickly
when moved from its own place.

IV
Vixens

Out the road, beyond our house
but not as far away as the shop,
a neighbour kept
a hissing vixen trapped in a rabbit hutch
in defiance of itself.

And I can hardly bear to talk about my mother.

Even the moon
wearing chiffon
over Lagan Lookout,

like some careworn
woman on a big night out,
reminds me of her.

V
Penance

A neighbour's child
was flung out
into the rain
at the back door
in her knickers and vest
like some heart-scald pup
in the process of house-training.

I'm a good girl Mama
Let me in! Mama! Mama!
Let me in!

What was it I did
that was so wrong
it was necessary
to fling me to my knees
before the Sacred Heart
to confess? To what?

I only remember being afraid,
because He could see me all the time
at any hour
and there was never any time off
from being good.

VI
Lifted Up

My brothers teased me
about the *looney-boy*—

what he wouldn't do when he caught me
because they'd make him.

The man in the shop said
What I wouldn't do with you if you were sixteen.

My legs would never carry
me fast enough

and my voice would never
squeal for me loud enough.

Who'd be there to hear me
but the man and the boy stopping in a Land Rover

to give me a lift on the road
when I had nowhere to go

and no need for a lift, anywhere—
only home?

VII
A State of Grace

Sleep with your arms crossed
across your chest

so you are ready
to meet God

if He comes for you
in the night.

VIII
Child

I could have stayed a child
forever, if I hadn't
been more terrified.

IX
Chrysalis

As though this part of me
belonged to someone else,

I left a skin

that didn't fit me any more
and dared to be loved.

X
Baptism

For the baptismal
Father Somethingorother
said that for as long as there was no marriage
there was no proof
whose daughter this was
and in the eyes of the law of God she would
   have no man's name,
no matter how she was registered, for that is a civic matter—
the Church would take no heed, no matter what
the law said or who had written it all and
who did I think I was to try and cover up my sinful life?
He would not be colluding with me,

a sinner.

I walked home under the rain
my sweet baby papoosed against my body
wondering about the sin it was to
occupy the house of God and call me

whore

liar

and my child

a bastard.

XI
Confirmation

At her Confirmation
the best that Bishop Farquhar
had to say was
how clever the boys were

and how these girls
should consider themselves lucky
to be sitting
beside their future husbands.

Well, I have daughters
to save them from all that.

They will not hang
on his words

and above all
never stand

in
the shadow
of him
or the likes
of him.

Flash Cards

There was always a fog in the P1 classroom—
Miss Morris was a chain-smoker.
Her desk nuzzled the cast iron stove
Johnny McCaffrey kept lit every day.

Flash cards. Dick and Dora
Nip and Fluff. Siobhan McKinney
knew her colours.
How could you ever know colours?

Later, after Bloody Sunday,
I tried to read the *Daily Mirror*
and work out what was happening
using the pictures as prompts—

bloodstains on the priest's hanky
in the Bogside from a world
no longer monochrome, even though
in our house, we weren't allowed to talk about it.

The Choreography of Being Pious

When Mother Peter developed full-blown
TB, we all had to have the vaccination
even if we never had music lessons,

even if we never had the knuckles
rapped off us with the long thin edge
of a wooden ruler.

They wouldn't do it now—
they couldn't get away with parading
six year olds past the desiccated

remnants of a parched Sister
of Mercy with her head bound
to keep her mouth shut,

coins on her eyes, cotton
stuffed up her nose.
See-no-evil, speak-no-evil.

We dared not make a sound;
I only pretended to touch her
and wouldn't breathe in.

Helen McCaffrey played piano.
She was holy, reverent—
knew the right moves.

I kept my eyes on her,
mimicking, unsteadily,
the choreography of being pious.

Imprint

At the Old Library Dr. Seuss
and *'The Cat in the Hat'*
were newcomers

the day I missed the bus
home and wet
my knickers

in the Gaol Square
in front of the teenagers
from the Tech.

Helen Corrigan
brought me home
to her mother

who, bless her,
brought me home
to my own mother.

Knees clenched, I sidled
as though I could
cover up the tell-tale cling

of a pink and white nylon
polka-dot frock
and the imprint

of the front page
of *The Impartial Reporter*
I had to sit on

to save the seat of the car.

Preparation for the Qually

Sister Sarto tickled us hard
and threatened to cut the gizzards out of us
if we didn't keep quiet.

She kept ostrich eggs,
old maps of the world, peacock feathers
and fossils in a glass press.

Forty-five voices droned
'Hail, Glorious St. Patrick',
'Be Thou My Vision',

'Soul of My Saviour'.
The Gestetner churned out
intelligence tests in purple ink.

But alone in the nuns' fusty tearoom
I boked into a clatty bucket
and listened to Gay Byrne.

For Anna, Aged 11

When your father died
you slept in his fleece
and clung to him
by the smell of him

until the ghosts took that too ...

Middle Eighths
for John

As varicose as a river at the edge of remembering
I am reaching for you,

we are standing off-centre,
facing up the steep slope of the back field.
Behind us, the side of the house
and the underline of the garage roof
frame Rossole Lough and Coleshill
as though they are the subject of this photograph—
not us, or the bluest sky.

The grass is not yet cut for hay;
I pull a skipping rope
tight to the back of my knees
and stand attention; you grin,
as if gormless, from underneath the thick
thatch of the barber-butchered fringe
you gifted yourself. We are children.

Other days are not trapped
in the light or in the inverse
imagery of a lens with a gloss finish—
the two of us, skiving off Mass
to midwife Sandy's pups in the piggery,
nesting them in a straw-stuffed trough;

or the hiding our mother gave us
for thieving cigarettes from Coulter's mobile grocery van.
How you laughed, punctuating
each thwack of rotten wood with a fart—
dancing round her grip on your wrist, like
a bucking bronco on a lasso.

Time was away ...
for Patricia

... down the loney on horseback to the lough.
Cowboys, 'pardners' side by side, ambling
on fat furry ponies with shabby tack
and no hats for safety.

From that height you could see
into the car passing: see the men
who held each other's penises,
(we didn't even know the word for penis then).

Families in black taxis
snaked through, over the border for the Twelfth,
their luggage and baby buggies
bursting from boots and roofs.

Slow down for horses
as one year welds to the next, season on season.
Bareback swimming in the Arney River—
no cure for sweet-itch.

Butch and Sundance.

Shadow Boxing

My father's feet
were hairy and hammer-toed.
He danced around
and shadow boxed
and started to skip in the backyard daily,
training for the 'Rumble in the Jungle'.

Dance with me, Daddy.
Let me stand on your feet.
Hold my hands when you
do that, and we'll move and shift
and duck and dive together.
Dance with me, Daddy.

Reading

We never knew
how you'd be

when you got home.
The dog either stayed

sharing the sofa
or dived for cover

under a table.
If he dived, we dived too—

in our house
you had to learn to read the dog.

Inflammable Material
after Stiff Little Fingers

come to. under the duvet. this Sunday morning
the clock a referee on countdown

Ten Nine Eight

i have spent all night on the canvas, vigilant,
half expecting someone to kick in the front door
or that a petrol bomb will announce its entry
to my orbit
in light,
heat
spangles of glass.

                    Surprise!   Surprise!

without warning i ricochet
off a south-paw
to the living room of 1974.

pungent cheese socks, a fog of cigarettes, whisky, a turf fire.

Ali bombaya!
Ali bombaya!
Ali bombaya!

i am on the floor. fast forward to the ropes

Emmanuel! Emmanuel!
the crowd heckle the Lord Mayor
he is Pilate in the *Life of Brian*
never mind Emanuel
never mind the Messiah

Seven Six
put the lights on
put the lights on days like this
Curtis Stigers' saxophone Van the Man

Five Four Three

Orla lies stock still
unblinking
staring into the cat's face

Sammy winked at me.
Sammy winked at me the way Bill Clinton winked at Aislín

she caught his eye
in a red duffle coat
when he threw her

a glance.

Two

One Lift off

one small step
for a man
Michael Collins stayed in
never dipped his toes
in the moon dust
Nixon Apollo zig zig Sputnik

& we never walk alone again
after my father meets Matt
Busby in the Gresham. All change
Blast Off we have Blast Off.

Sunday paras. strike

Ulster Workers' Council. strike
petrol shortages, strike
we have no milk
wehavenomilk

THIS IS A POLICE MESSAGE

would all key-holders in the area of Cross Street Enniskillen
please return to their premises, immediately, where
    a suspect device ...

Mary-Con Maguire McManus
keeps *knockin' life out*
to keep knockin' life in
& supervises the making of soup
on Bunsen burners in the science lab of the boys' school
we will not close our kitchens
not one foot
if we have to knit the lunches we will do it
we shall overcome the point
at which gelignite Molotov
internment Sunningdale
assassination sub-machine gun
armybombdisposalunits
and saracen enter
the lexicon of Scrabble

we give up playing
cowboys and Indians for secret armies

one man one vote early vote often
decades disappear in smithereens

i sold Harry West a raffle ticket at the airshow in St. Angelo
1st prize was a pony he said he didn't want but he bought
    a ticket anyway
saying he never won anything
asking did I not know
who he was when i went to write out the stub
    and suggesting
i ask Douglas Bader. he was visiting.

flying boats. sinking the Bismarck

i do not win the pony either but my father buys a mare—
her show name *Say Nothing*

my sister and brother go to Blue Lamp discos
    in the High School

does anyone know the way?
there's got to be a way,

                    to blockbuster

during breaktime we read
Lace and *Emmanuelle*
in the maths storeroom & sing new songs
Debbie Harry's heart of glass the tide is high we are holding
on when the RUC arrive in the 6th form common room
to arrest suspects of impersonation

we can smell the blankets from here
comms on Rizlas
Ireland unfree

we don't know Portora boys but call them wasps
nothing personal

what we need is an Alternative Ulster
what we need, is an alternative, Ulster

Sister Una sends Edel McElholm to
the principal's office for pretending
she is Soupdragon out of the Clangers
making blue string pudding
while standing on the bench
in chemistry
amusing us all when the nun
is late for class. Again.

i build a tunnel from the library to anywhere
as surreptitiously as the men in *The Great Escape*
& smuggle the soils out in my pockets
i walk them into the gutters
but it is all blown up in advance of its own official
opening—the school windows ajar
so they can take the blast
& stay unbroken in the aftermath

when is a door not a door
reach throw wade row

i keep my head down and don't
go to Ginn's (much) for chips & cigarettes—
one coke and aspirin. 6 straws.

i collect the family
allowance and shop for groceries
but not in Lipton's anymore (too dear)
i get the late bus

to the control zone of home-
made barricades & Christmas
shoulder to shoulder

ourselves
alone

unable to offer each other
the sign of peace.

on another bloody Friday or was it Saturday
my father is watching the *Late Late*
Conor Cruise O'Brien is Gaybo's guest
get me that bollocks on the phone

ring RTE
ring his house
phone the exchange
get his number off directory enquiries
ring the operator
no—
i don't want to talk to his wife
tell her
to tell him
he has to ring me
the minute he gets home
for he knows nothing
nothing about what is goin' on up here

nothing

the phone spills its guts onto the stairs again
its umbilicus spent
cut off from the placenta of STC
ripped out & flung
like a hand grenade. in trenches.

it is another other Sunday
i am leaving home

at last, in my aunt's
spluttering car with

its broken radio

divert off the motorway at the Maze

                    stop

do not pass go
do not go to jail
do not collect ...
what is your name
what is your date of birth
where are you going to
where are you coming from
what is the purpose of your journey
what have you got in the bag

suspicious package, incendiary. a security search

if we'd known better we could have said
38 fish suppers

for the craic

don't believe her
don't believe her
don't be bitten twice
got a suss suss suss suss
suss suss suss

suspect device.

Swan Song 1

His eyes are a flick-knife.
His nose is a conspiracy.
His teeth are dredgers scavenging the bed
of a dead city river.
His breath is a pollution of acid.
His neck is a vice—winding, winding.
His shoulders are gallows.
His arms are more razor wire
at the margins of a concentration camp
after I thought I'd escaped already.
His fingers are splinters of chicken bone
wedged at the back of my throat.
His heart is a mercury tilt switch.
His stomach is hell's blazing poultice.
His skin is nuclear fallout for chromosomes.

And for all that,
it is hard
to stay staying away.

Beyond Waking
For Louis

Him
lying there. Rouged for Chrissakes!
Like some sick joke
or revenge, in Virgin Mary blue
and a white satin dickey-bow.

I slid the orange pompom
woolly-feathered beaky birds the children made,
in beside his waxy manicured hands
and the rosary beads,
and thought of boats
the ancients gave the dead
to ferry them to the other world.

In my dreams
he moved silently, night-weary as absolution,
though everywhere was broken:
shattered glass;
men in balaclavas;
someone else's children stealing cars;
dancing in warehouses;
pushing the button—

self destruct, self destruct—

while he cooked breakfast
and slipped out the back door
to tell stories.

There was nothing else to do.

Things coalesced
in disorder,
out of tune, out of place, out of time.
I fumbled
in my pockets, in my sleep,
all night, night on night,
never finding that something
beyond the torn lining
of my best work suit,
and spent the days in a chair,
unmoving, in case the house
would notice
and devour me.

I walked the streets
when only the moon was out
wondering if maybe, just maybe,
if I could think hard enough
I could make him come
back, or send me a sign from the other
world he told me that he knew was there
without a doubt.

* * *

Later, much much later
something would catch in my eye
or slip into my breathing,
puncture me
from offside
and I'd be
blubbering: at the sink;
opening the door to the builder;
or once, driving into a checkpoint

of bewildered squaddies
at dawn.

That summer
great swatches of
dog daisies
showered
the steep banks
to the roadside.
The world would
give me this one
indulgence—
to fill the
car with them

like some crazy hearse
disappearing
rapidly
in the wrong
direction

so I could
breathe again
and be gone.

Swan Song 2

Still.
I would rather
bear these amputations
show these sores, these scars.
I would rather carry this than hide
like some ringed, tagged,
clipped, grounded
eunuch of a bird
that looks the part
but is more broken.

On Hatfield Street

They caught my eye—
this abundance of flowers,
this two-fingered gesture
to the death throes of winter,
the sun's insult to the dark.

And I remember
the stonemason's fall—
his fist gone flaccid,
leave-loose the beaten docket
under the drum roll.

I still have
the stone slab
of white marble
destined for a headstone:
the chill it holds
is good for working pastry,
(though we rarely
have the heart.)

At night we'd hear
him doing 'homers',
chipping out messages
the living give the dead.

And there were times
buzzards from the gasworks
purged the sidestreets
of vermin, after the storms,
when floodwater
near brought the river
to the foot of the stairs.

Under cover of darkness
every house in the district
had a note pushed
through the letterbox.

Let that be a warning.

I always slept 'with one ear on the street'
and my stomach turns over, remembering
the car revving,
shattering glass, spraying shots
its tyres squealing: I heard
someone else's children crying.

Too afraid to put the lights on
or look out round the curtains
or use the phone or go to sleep
or be awake and hear what I was hearing,
I clung to my baby, praying
it was no-one I knew, and
that by morning I would still
know nothing.

Tit for tat.
More dead posies on a lamp post.

They say Big Johnny
must have said something out of line, that he
got somebody's back up
in the *Vatican City*.
Somebody decided
he should be taken out.
That would be enough to justify
grown men wrapping themselves
in carpet and diving
through the living room

window at 3 o'clock
in the morning
with guns in their hands.

We thought me Da
had gone stone mad
the night
he tore
through our room
and pulled our very beds
over in front of the door,
before he jumped out the upstairs window,
and escaped to the neighbours.

We buried our screams
like depth charges.

When her dog went missing
a woman round the corner called the peelers

I'll be raped in my bed without that dog,
I'll be raped in my bed.

They wouldn't walk the district calling him home:
Here Fenian! Here boy! C'mon Fenian.

It must have been the only dog
not called Rebel.
Displaced from the country, I recall our dog was Santa:
for a time, we'd been innocent along the Border.

When the boyo up the street
was caught on camera
nicking eggs
out of the Shell garage

on the front of the road,
they wound him up
something shocking:
they decked the whole pub out with egg boxes
so they did—
put a round of questions
all about it in the pub quiz,
so they did.

A stray woman
wrote Ry Cooder
on the walls
of the Holylands
and stole cold cats
off the window-sills
of other people's houses
and went hungry
to feed them.

Dolores was back on the juice again
she was clean out of men:
clean out of sorrow.
She had a hop-a-long uneven
scoliosis kind of limp-thing going on
even when she was sober.

She had too-black hair
and drew her eyebrows on:
she called my Kevin, Caobhín
even though she had a Caobhín of her own
and chose to call him Kevin.

Our neighbour's son
was shot dead 'over the bridge'
walking to work in a supermarket.

After that she kept
an Alsatian dog
in a back yard the size of a grave:

there's not much room left
when you build
a 2-storey extension on a 2-up 2-down

over the space where
the privy used to be.
He barked non-stop, but only

all night: so that's not
so bad then.
She got the dog to feel safe:

she said she felt
more secure.
What the dog was going to do

locked in the back yard
3-6-5, I'll never know, but he
howled at the moon for her

so she didn't have to.

Somebody else was shot in the bar
at the corner.
A man just walked in
off the street
and blew another man's brains out
all over the place.

At the time
there were that many barriers

you could hardly get in
to the pub.

Buzz the door.   Speak to an intercom.

              Look for a camera

Step in.   Wait.   Step in.

But the houses were cheap
and I needed a roof over my head
and anyway,
with the cricket ground at the back
and a view over the river
to the Ormeau Park at the front,
there were times
you could have believed you were
anywhere.

And I brought a child into this.

The council built 'the reccy'
at the river
but refused to put
a play park
on the waste ground.
They said they couldn't put it there:

too close to the river
too dangerous

So they didn't put it anywhere
and never came to fix
the holes in the fence
and didn't care

when somebody's child
was *one stone more, that dark stone,*
the pure stone which the river bears away.

We left before the place
came under siege—
and, semi-detached,
half a mile further up the road,
I watched the drama
unhinge on the television,
then I stood in the street with David and Ivy
talking about rights and wrongs,
the Battle of the Somme
and if ever we could protect each other
even if we wanted to.

Down the road
the people couldn't take it any more
after 'themmins' danced past—
five nil, five nil.
Waving their hands
five nil.

So the RUC and the army
cordoned off the whole place
and pass laws came
to the Lower Ormeau Road.

You had to have I.D.
to get in to your own home
and climb out
over the bonnet of a jeep
to leave your own front door
to go for milk.

To his eternal shame
(although he doesn't know it yet)
The Right Honourable Reverend Martin Smith M.P. said:

It's their own fault,
these Roman Catholics,
encroaching up the Ormeau Road
from the Markets.

I am too close in
to the heart of *my* explosion,
I am neither here nor there:
there is *always* only a hurry
through which known and strange things pass.

Rock the baby.
Rock the baby all night
perched
on the precipice
on a bed.

These shreds of poppies
fill my eyes with sting.

Whatever you say
say nothing

and keep on saying it.

All Changed, Changed Utterly
Easter 2002

A deaf rent-boy stopped us in a back street
near the Cathedral, blaggin' cigarettes and company.
Tellin' us his life story. Everything

from the head injury he *caught*
in a fall from a flat in Lenadoon,
to the dead parents dyin' in a house fire,

and the money he earns in the brothel of a sex shop to
supplement the DLA.
He's the pretty-boy nephew of a drag queen

who wears an inflatable band with a cleavage
for boobs, under a bra top.
He wants to buy a camp yellow Mini

with the money he gets from the claim for his fall
and a flat of his own,
so his boy can't lock him out.

How he doesn't do drugs.
How his trousers aren't the cleanest.
How he puts his make-up on.

Later, we talked about safe sex,
heroin in Belfast,
downsides of the peace process

and we stopped for chips on the way home.

An Emotional Argument Defies Logic

I
Her-Story

I cannot push back this slick of filth—
things here are no more satisfying or valid
than a life spent plucking out every hair
from my own body, day in, day out, one by one.

I am all turned in—
bloated under the weight of a four-day binge of chocolate
with nothing better to show for it than the penury
of cleaning the grill pan. Again.

There is nothing the matter in this relationship
that a 'new' man, equality and sharing the workload
wouldn't sort out once and for all.
But I am a sucker for the belief

that it is more important for the children
to have a good father, than that
a wife needs a good husband, as though
at heart, they are not really the same thing anyway.

And tomorrow

to demonstrate how reconstructed and reformed you are,
you will wash up your own cereal bowl and spoon, but
leave everything else to sit and congeal—a scab
in the crack of a joint, reopening with every small movement.

II
His-Story

Tonight I lay here dreaming—fantasising
about making love to you, but instead
I have ended up with an in-depth analysis
of the significance of an icebucket, its place in the room
(at the time) in relation to you
and a single offhand comment
that maybe you could get it yourself.

According to you, I had missed the part
where you had secured the table,
garnered an extra chair,
ferried the drinks from the bar
and were only asking for a favour.
Apparently, it wasn't about ice anyway
but being cared for, attended to.

I don't understand women—never asking
for what they want (attention)
but by metaphor (ice) .

III
Her

So how did we get here? To the point
where squalor perpetuates itself, replicating
like a virus—where the grubs
on the glass in this door between us
are only marked with smudged lips and the imprint
of your nose
from when you squashed against it,
in your court jester way, as if blowing kisses.

I see only a dirty window.

It is me—this house. I am it.
It's not as if I haven't told you that before
and even though you say that you believe me—
nothing changes.
The dirty laundry breeds and soon
there will be no option
but for the world to see it.

IV
Them

And any bed becomes a battleground
for a turf war that is a dance; a ritual
somewhere between familiarity,
contempt, satisfaction or boredom. Choices.

There must have been a time

We really loved each other once (yes)

When—you remember—skin on skin (yes)

Heat (yes)

We shared the one breath (yes)

Smells (yes)

Eyes (yes)

Yes (yes)

We didn't know our scripts were different then.
That the back-story was riddled
with gaping holes,
frayed edges, old wounds.

Because it looked like stars, or
like the moon on water. It tasted
like chocolate, smelled of honey-

suckle.

V
Comparing

Every morning early. Too early.
They made their way up Candahar Street
from the Annadale Flats, to the Ormeau Park.

She wore a duffle coat, a too-short
skirt, no tights, matching black eyes
inch-long grey roots in her hair.

He wore a bomber jacket, a skinny under-
fed frame, piss-stained trousers,
his three-piece of need.

Her pocket bulged with the makings
of a hangover it didn't seem worth
crawling out from under,

and we had the cheek to call them
the happy couple.

VI
A View From the Duffle Coat

They're smug them pair,
look at them! Hand in hand—and particular!

He never lets her gather flowers.
The park is full of daffodils this time of year—

and yet, he won't even let her
take the broken ones the dogs have tossed.

There's a place for flowers—
and that is in the ground.

My eyes are only blackened—I'm not blind,
I see enough to know the shine wears off.

When Juliet stops singing from the bandstand
it will end in tears.

Seeing Red

My eyes are hungry for the colour red.
I need it as I need water.
On this tipping point of autumn, I scan the landscape
for vivid radiance—
finding it
in scattered splashes
like touches of fresh pillar-box—
a signature.

I buy lipstick,
hunt out tones in hydrangeas, garage doors,
wine, teething-baby cheeks, my neighbour's
    window-boxed geraniums,
ruby resin door handles in my old house,
the *Sacred Heart Messengers* my grandmother saved for me.

I put lilies in the living-
room for scent and feed my eyes
on carnations, late roses, my notebook,
a cardigan, blush, tomatoes,
out of season berries. It is there
in the smells of cinnamon,
cloves, blackcurrants, and plums. Apples.

In my dreaming, a tower, Agent
Orange, famines, rats and desert storms invade; and
I know red is searching for me too.

Lunchtime with Rosie
For Kevin and for Rosie

I

I am dreaming of the miracle of your face;
curves; eyes, lips—
it comes to me in fragments;
the image is not whole. Your smile. Still.

The Cannonau Riserva was too like a port wine,
too strong; a titration
into blue notes I didn't know were there. Waiting.
I wrapped into a blanket on the roof terrace,
watched the sun sink and the moon rupture the dark—
there is the sea,
                        ripping and repairing itself in waves.

Jacaranda, bougainvillea, hollyhocks, cacti, geranium,
figs, peaches, pomodori, plumbago, lovers in the water.

The builders roof the new apartment block,
blocking the view, housing it in concrete
and still everything is blue. Mrs House-proud next door,
waters the garden
twice a day every day
while torpor insists itself into the heat, mocking a life
driven by not enough, not good enough, not long enough,
not paid enough,
not perfect enough.

In the mountains, far up
in the mountains, cork oaks, stripped to the waist,
red-rusted, bleeding, are at work;
wild myrtle, languid, thickens the air,

so I can taste it just by breathing.
Butterflies, cicadas, dragonflies,
ants, dust and tiny blue flowers;

    olive trees.

II

We sit here together
sifting the dance steps and snapshots of our lives;
our daughters; our compound fractures of homes
like mirror images; the state of our world,
wars, the weather and whether
these olives are for sharing:
We know punk rebellions set us free
and we don't want to die.

Postpartum Weather Reports

Everything is overcast and heavy,
maybe there will be rain later.

A storm comes with the waters' break,
a breech birth folding me: plate tectonics

at a fault line in the earth-crust
I straddle; a world shattering now

forever; all the ocean's salt is not enough
to clean the rottenness from these wounds;

my spirit is rewired all wrong.
Splintered synapse codes deflect

the smothering clay dust
of a fallen forbidden city:

wash away, wash away. Let me walk
backwards into the sea—

my salt: its salt, angels whisper
at the blue windows of heaven.